Books by Howard Moss

Buried City

Buried City

Poems by Howard Moss

New York Atheneum 1975

Grateful acknowledgment is made to the following magazines in which these poems first appeared: THE NEW YORKER: *Chekhov, The Old Poet, Sawdust, Three Winter Poems, Bay Days, Nearing the Lights, The Stairs, Saratoga, At the Masseur's, Tropical Fish, Travel: A Window, Buried City, Morning, Night, and Very Late, Tattoo, Winter Botany, On Route 202, New Hampshire, Memories of Lower Fifth, Anemones, Shorelines;* POETRY: *Magic Affinities;* ESQUIRE: *Cold-Water Flats;* THE COLUMBIA FORUM: *Hunting and Fishing;* ATLANTIC MONTHLY: *Someone;* THE IOWA REVIEW: *After the Ballet.*

For Robert Mazzocco

Contents

V

I

Chekhov

We have the whole evening ahead of us,
We think, our eyesight starting to weaken,
We must have missed the houselights growing dim,
But how could that moment have escaped us when
The roots of the paper trees struck water
And transformed themselves into the real thing—
This nervous wood at the edge of a small,
Provincial town whose still-lifes waken
To find that they're portraits after all
And subject to the risk of animation?

Tonight we may discuss—after the Chopin
Nocturnes, after the I-don't-know-how-many
Performances of Beethoven's "Moonlight" Sonata—
The gradual reduction of Roman columns,
The disease of too many lakes and clouds.
Do cobblestones have a future? Is rain
Removeable? Depressing mornings find
Characters in bed who have no reason
To get up, the light a yellowish half-light
Mirroring the mind, its sad affections.

At the lake, a flat of faultless summer
Is being taken down, the view abandoned;
The puzzled players change their places. Once
You might have found them walking in an orchard,
The blossoms opening their mouths to speak
And song occurring as if it were natural;
Now that trees uproot themselves and bankrupt
Agriculture wanes in its drying furrows,

Property and battlefields turn out to share
A fate in common—they exchange hands.

Shrines "fallen out of the perpendicular,"
Stones "that have apparently once been tombstones"—
We are on someone's estate not far from Moscow.
How simply the sun goes out like a match!
How deeply the wounds stay on the surface!
He said the best that can be said for property:
It lets an old man fall in love with landscape,
Lets so many trees have a chance to be noticed,
Allows the self-interested birds to preen,
Until the property is lost again

To an upstart creditor who sells the trees
For lumber, then, to the sound of saws,
Tramps through the hallway in his dirty boots
To explain, in tears, the dreary motivation:
His mother's dying, his young wife's in love
With a boor. . . . The Babel of trouble starts;
Among all the hells that go on talking,
Only one is real, though it is silent,
And everything leads up to it—to lose
The land, to lose the very ground you stand on.

If the temporary brilliancies gather once more
In the middle distance, and the modal lark
Persuades the summer evening to reveal
One private little splendor not for sale,
Still, a gunshot, onstage or off,

4

Tells us what no one is prepared to know:
Love is a tourniquet tightening its bands
Around the slowly dying wrist of freedom,
Futility's a spinster bending over
A book of household accounts forever.

Bathed in the acid of truth, all things
Become possible: to be a cold snake
At an interview, to live on scraps of soap
To keep oneself warm, to resemble a cat
Constantly stalking the shadow of nothing.
To the horse's clop-clop outside the window,
Or the sound of a guitar from a neighboring room,
The doctor, with a smile, asks, What is man?
A hero about to be done-in for good?
A villain about to be rescued by pain?

The governess is wearing her old forage cap.
That's Epihodov playing his guitar.
Astrov is talking about trees. We could be
Racing the wolves at thirty below
In a ravine whiplashed by snow, or slowly
Succumbing to boredom in a seaside town,
Waiting for a future that will never be,
The heat getting worse, far off the waves
Pounding faintly late in the moonlight,
At a low moment in our lives.

II

Morning, Night, and Very Late

1

So vulnerable the merest
Water drop
Could kill a song cycle,
The birds have taken up
Their posts, the first
Subversives of the day,
Who chirp the light
Into position,
Instinct on a thread . . .

2

Cutting the lamps off, flicking the radio
On, or off, the blinds attended to,
Something is building up in the empty
Fireplace, something that long ago burned there—
Is it the old love that no longer answers
The phone, a mail key dropped through a sewer
Grating, the address on a packet of matches
You're wild to find but cannot remember?

3

I'm in a bar I thought I'd forgotten,
The wings of the jukebox flying, flying,
Trumpets—is it blood that is silver?—
In a dance palace, down by the river.

Memories of Lower Fifth

1

I loved them once, those towering hotels
On lower Fifth, where I imagined lives
Far richer than those lives turned out to be:
Snow linen and the corollary warmth
Of fires screened away from rare, old rugs,
The ping of knives, the smell of morning coffee,
Crystal, silk, polished mahogany—
The world cut off by plush and drapery.

2

I saw façades become the ruins they hid,
The usual drift of class, of style to none,
A genteel century of fireplaces
Teeter in the air, the wrecker's ball
Swing back in space to slam in once again
Against the dangling painting of a wall
To bring another room down to its floor,
Another floor down to another floor.

3

One snowy winter night, the traffic lights
Shed small circles every block or two
And made of bell-resounding streets a town
Blind faith constructed in a magic mirror.
Such were the slopes, the signs, the gradients
I rode into countries of the zodiac
Past the north scarps of French-speaking mountains
Onto stopped carpets of an English square.

Tattoo

The fountain-pen bird has punctured the vein
Of the sea and nests in a pool of muscle,
Is borne into the dark pulse of a nipple,
Scratching its way across phonograph records,
Wanting its fix of a photograph taken
Long ago. The darkroom is waiting

For a green-scaled dragon brought from the South Seas
To lick away all the animal islands;
It's sometimes smaller or larger but always
Green, its red tongue flicking in effort,
Winding its way up to the armpit. . . .

Think of these: rinses, makeup, ampules,
A dressing room blooded by Band-Aids of healing,
Eye-pencilled alphabets, ink blots of jungle,
A gypsy tearoom run by a surgeon,
A beaded curtain, a paintbox, a sudden
Movement of pain, the animal willfully
Formed at the end of a point, a child's stencil.

Alcohol taxies the sailor at midnight
To the empty street at the docks, the tugs lowing;
Under a blue bulb's eye in the doorway,
The leopard of self, clawing at neon,
Begins to yearn for the ritual scarring
Of the Cupid of wounds, its arrowed citation.

Look how the snake is emerging from hiding,
The taut bow bending its string to the arrow,

A gallery plunged under skin to remember
Rose of Torquay, Malaya, Belinda. . . .
Fleets of Chicago, membranes of Newport,
All night the dye-needle branding its stories
Into the flesh to be told there forever.

Someone

You watch the night like a material
Slowly being crammed into a tube of rooms;
It showers into gunshot, pepper, dew,
As if a hand had squeezed it at one end,
Is blank as innocence when daylight comes
Projecting sunlit patches on the wall
That fade. Too much is going on, too much
Of life, you say, for you to live alone
On top of an old tenement, on a train
That might start off sometime, but never does.
Your view is gone. Turn around, and boom!,
A park appears between two fixed ideas
Whose narrow aperture of sky in time
Will house the slums of 1989 . . .

Now New York is feigning its gray dark
London winter. Invisible uptown
Is out there somewhere, raining on its own.
Palmed in the dusty pane, a circle bares
A scene that seems reprinted from the past:
A man with a dog is walking very fast
Along a path among the stunted trees
Of the little square below. He disappears.

Winter Botany

1

You can hear the dogs
At the edge of town.
It's fall. The hills
Are slowly filling up with spinster sculpture—
Before the whole *mise en scène* collapses,
How can we explain our devotion to
The second rate,
Our three false languages:
Government, medicine, and law?

2

Who put those malteds in the sea
And the angels in alphabetical files?
The mail piles up for the departed,
The insipid surprises of middle life
Pile up, when what we wanted were
Tame lions with musicians in a royal park,
Extracts of smoke, the lunch of ages,
Undying moonlight fettered at the feet
Of prima ballerinas crammed with poems,
Whose net impact would be marvelous . . .

3
Instead what we got was a century
Good for poems but not for poets, talk
Reduced to small talk, grunts among the trees
Heralding the terrors of the lapsed thing:
Days whose events refused to happen,
Money lost before we could count it,
Nights of unrecollected being.

4
Night sweats and stomach cramps,
Their symptoms set the tone
In this city of four million love affairs
That has its night life on
And divides the world into two great camps:
The mad great, and the not great mad;
In dreams we find ourselves alone,
Looking down from a high wire,
With no net below,
Thinking we know one truth at least:
Not to be loved is to crave power.

The Old Poet

"I had forgotten how the book once read
Before I rewrote it, how the letters jumped
Onto the blankest of white pages, how
A change of light and sound for every day
Traced my world inside its tracery,
How the pages, turning in the wind,
Were first a lexicon of light, of leaves
Drenched in nothing but themselves before
The word for leaves gave birth to more than leaves,
The word for light made possible more light
Before sleep took the very word for word
And drowned it back into a pool so wide
Its underground of nerves lay everywhere.

"The morning gradually rose. I rose,
Fed by a luminous transparency
That led the azure down on steps of cloud
To where I stood before a window open
Wide upon a thousand worlds I thought
I knew. Five stories slapped themselves awake.
Then a thousand. Faces took their forms
And drilled them deep into my weathered eyes.
Now I can tell a story of my own;
It is a book I read again, again—
Not the great long novel of my heart
But the one slim volume it has all become."

Cold-Water Flats

A RAILROAD FLAT

The meanest melon slice of sunlight rims
An olive velvet unmade daybed, dims
Out of its own accord along the sides
Of a kitchen bathtub, hesitates, and then
Shivers for a second, and goes down the drain.
Two windows always face a tiny square
Of neon signs and grass—Hopper? Sloan?
Loneliness is like the upper floor
Of a house like this, where you live alone,
And downstairs somebody is always home.

TWO BAYS

A cardboard on its back, perforated by
A thousand little syphons, that's the bay—
Or was before the tide turned. Oysters caught
Their breath for miles around, and we caught them,
Bare-handed, barefoot, on cold-water flats.
That was Wellfleet. Now it's Gardiners Bay.
It's fishy here, and an unhappy place,
Or let's say we are. The fish factory's
Defunct. It squats like an abandoned town
That's lost its one and only industry.

WIND INSTRUMENTS

Sharps and flats. You need wind instruments
To play them, notes you never heard before,
Asleep between the strict piano keys.
They're lovelier than brains, what songbirds sing,
I mean blues singers singing after dark
Mid-Eastern scales through open windows—songs
That streak into the blood, are ready when
You least expect them on the sounding board,
And bring back taxi lights in rain, the inks
Of summer, its black lights, and golden tans.

WINDOWS

Another dumb enchanter out of gas,
I pass your house and look up in the dark;
You aren't home, or are asleep, I guess.
Blank bandages still waiting for their wounds,
The windows rise in tiers. As slow fog creams
Up from the river, sleepers turn their dreams
Into clichés come true. Who hasn't had
His private little hell? Oh, yes. Mine was
Those months of pain no one could see me through.
Not that you loved me. Or I loved you.

Tropical Fish

Velvet sulphur powder puffs, and cream
And lavender arrangements trimmed with ice,
Little chandeliers and pulsing lanterns,
Lipstick streaks, and ermined eyes of gin
Shaken in cut glass, and sleighs of Roman
Stripes, and azure mirrors under skin,
Bones like silk embedded in a crystal,
Armor made of mica, gilded wine
Strung like buoys along a throbbing wire,
Snows collecting into white jade bulges,
Milktails of successive pale blue arches
Stippling into gray, G-clef signs
Descending slowly on their licorice threading—
Glass and waterglass, rain on rain.

Sawdust

Open, doll. Switch off your golden hair.
Unzip the cross-stitched seam at the base there
And let the pale, crushed monitors float free.
Look at the empty wooden interior,
Solid but fragile, a fingernail of skull . . .
You can break it apart like a piece of candy.
Open, open up. Mr. Sesame is here,
Miss Thorazine in tight gold velvet tights,
And Thomas Edison, inventing night life—
Aren't they a winsome, gruesome threesome?
They clash, dash forward with their curving knives,
Circling toward the two bull's eyes ahead,
And out they go through two polestars of light.

2

Out to what? Did I say night life?
Septic dusk, the nets about to fall,
The silky excitement of a gypsy movie,
Magic cranked out of the ordinary:
Crowds—what crowds!—illusionary people!
Each, a silent telegram, goes by.
Satisfied hungers no longer suffice.
Here: two lovers translating each other.
Here: a schoolroom balanced on a cliff.
There: a street of epical negation—
Clothes that fall apart, food that cannot nourish.
(Only cheap places can pay the high rent now.)
The smog is trying to become more lucid.

3
Out of commission, gears mesh with anything.
Or rust. Sometimes it comes in cycles, say,
A little bit of both: frenzy and resting.
Violence pours from the vat of rejection
As if destruction were displaced affection.
Look at a tree. Then at the sawdust floor
Of one of those decorated, gimcrack places
That mimic the taste of the turn of the century.
Though you can't see it, you know the connection.
So get the matches and the needles ready,
The chains, the belts, the paraphernalia—
The bulging, red-eyed children plunge again
Into the powerless mirrors of power,
Still wondering, as the gearshifts move,
If pain is a substitute for love, or love.

III

At the Masseur's

1

Entering at first, body in mind,
I hadn't noticed the rug at all,
Its suède-green heron splayed against
Sky-blue, angora of light, a plush
Sand beach whose total afternoon
Unmitigated summer rocks with blue,
Savannas of weedy acres, winged
Needle-darters, nervous at the shore. . . .
This hallway's sensual stained red glass
In a leftover brownstone's leaded door,
My feet sinking into pile, I move
Obediently up the gloomy stairs.
Indoor pool? Cool funeral parlor?
Who else lay here, who else will lie?
The warp must go, all flesh is sand. . . .

I notice, body, you begin to end.

2

Undressed, pummelled, stroked, caressed,
What do the nerves still grant to touch
Alone? Probably everything:
Tension unmoors a ghost of ease whose nerves
Race backward through the wash of years to one
Not quite recapturable afternoon
When power was in *my* hands . . . a green room
Of waves advancing, a chorus line
Of gulls, the shore's wet sand an ore
Dribbled like icing from a pastry tube

Onto the rising towers of a castle
The ocean crumbled—tunnel, arch, and moat;
Collapsing parapets melted into sea,
The shadow of a child withdrew into
A shingled house. . . .
                              My body's struck anew
Under the studied cunning of a hand
Equally skilled at feather, silk, or steel.
Is this the stuff that Donatello knew,
Whose marble draperies could stir the wind?
Stone muscle, sinew, lion-limb that grew
Under the hands of Michelangelo?

Rodin! Your thinker is not thinking now!

I eagerly give up to a sensation known
In childhood: well-being flooding through
The body's alleyways whose hunched-up pain
New pressure slakes into a milk and dew:
Atlantic motion, Caribbean lull,
Beach umbrella, suntan lotion, shoe
Removed so foot may shape itself in sand,
Natural pleasure issues from the hand
Of . . .
           of a masseur who plays an instrument
Relaxed into the harp it meant to be,
And I asleep upon the table, or
Dreaming it, emerging from the water,
Walk across the flashing yarns and edges
Of a carpet spread before the sea, whose border

3
Knits itself of thread,
Sinking foam, crêpe-paper,
Underfoot, instead
Of a heron a sandpiper—

The sheet is a sand beach,
That purring motor hum
Vibrator, tidal lurch . . .
Shaken, the waves come.

The body's second birth:
A Greek god Time undoes.
Now we are going north,
Landlubbers on a cruise,

To pines, lakes, motels;
Crawling through crumbling jade,
We snake up molded hills,
The late light lemonade . . .

In New Hampshire twilight,
A swimmer streaks from shore
Out to his little float—
Square rug going threadbare . . .?

One summer, rectitude
Deserted me, half ill,
I took bread at the hand
Of a beggaring, sexual,

Illiterate command—
Bitter, obsessive summer!
Only flesh could mend . . .
Let's draw the veil of kind-

ly darkness over . . .

4
Slack and stress, first pressure and then none,
This life-saver revives his drowning man.
Aware of sound—a radio kept low—
I wake to see the curtains blow their cool,
A black cat pouncing on the daybed, my
White shirt a brand-new patchwork for its joy.

It's over. I get up. We talk. I dress.
A painting hangs beside an odd recess
That houses a small sculpture: *David*? No,
But something similar: a discus thrower
Revived from grammar school. Poor Miss Lafour
Who mastered Art but not the art of dress . . .
The whole affair takes no more than an hour. . . .
I say I'll call again. Then pay. And go.

5
How much I hide! Art's overcoats
Cover the naked figure seen.
Time takes them up, the rugs, the floats,
All places where the body's been.

"The figure in the carpet . . ." Henry James.
Time is at the loom. With a final stitch,
The design unravels. Memory blooms:
The past, the present. Who knows which is which?

"I was touched," someone later that night
Remarks. And so was I. I see
At last the long drawn-out conceit:
Body. The sea. The Medici . . .

6
Kings have wept to know the frame of art
Is fleshless, soul lifting out of bone. . . .
Mind, you are singular, the heart stops
At the splendor of the young who all too soon
Drink up their ambience, eat out the heart
Of every age whose business is to kill
That blooming apricot, that clavicle
So moving it seems more pure than all
The dancer's moving light, even when still.

IV

The Stairs

Starting out as love, it climbed the stairs,
And then came down as something else again;
I did not recognize its killing features
Until I saw they were my very own.

Tonight, the babbling ghost of the remains
Sits in a room of starlight and of snow;
The owl tests its meretricious brains
Against the winter, and what comes back slow

Is the oldest sound that ever shook these hills,
The train's iron echo. Silence, its white bear,
States and restates a sentiment that kills:
Claws absolute. And plain. And everywhere.

Hair I remember, and lips like prizes,
The fluent eyes' divinities and, bare,
The flaring hollows of newborn surprises,
The clearest of all sleeps, then nothing clear.

Anemones

Your waxen petals'
    Upturned cups,
Each with a spider
    At the center,
Have stems with beads
    Of pollen like
A honey drop
    Hung from a spike,
Or soft wool fiber,
    Black, erect,
Powdery, wet,
    Yet delicate.

Widening
    Your heavy oils
Into fine satiny
    Wings and wheels
Of fire fused
    On insect legs,
Are you the eyes'
    Lasting look
At nothing, nothing
    Before it sees
At last
    Nothing but anemones?

Magic Affinities

The Muse disseminated wisdom's music:
"Three," she announced, "is the way of magic—
If you can arrange the same words three ways . . ."
GEORGE TREMPLAR

I

You, the lady of magic affinities,
Know how appetite grows larger on
What starves it. Such lovely days
Are lovely days for love, I could write,
And lie. Pleasures, complacencies,
Are habits remaining serviceable.
I am tired, yes. But not of you.

Evil arrives in the guise of the pitiful.
The dancers' synthetic intensity
Blurs the stony difference between
Desire and desire. Today the sea
Is filled with old Elizabethan plays . . .

Liar! The sunset's gravity reveals
Antonyms of green—sky-mirrors and delights,
The astrological swan, and others:
Sculpture, coliseums, coins, ourselves.
We were. We are. We will not be.
Each river has a town, each town a river;
Along its banks, it palms its treasuries:
Forms of knowledge, such as gravel, grass,
Sticks, stones, and light flotillas of the weed,
But, up in our houses, our nature is to fight

Nature.
    Lady, only arrive.

2

When we were complacent it was pleasureable,
But lady, that gravel is not grass on which
You bank your magic affinities
Grown larger on what starved them. I could write
We were ourselves the way the green takes light
Or rivers mirror towns, but evil arrives,
Blurring the difference between the sea
And the sunset. Remaining light reveals
The swan as a dancer of intensity
Whose antonyms—of gravity, delight—
Although synthetic, are still antonyms
Of coins whose serviceable habits lie,
Palmed treasuries in coliseum banks.

We fight the lovely days of love, and lie.
Desire is an old Elizabethan play,
A mirror of indifference because it is,
And was, and will be other than ourselves.
You know the sticks and stones of appetite
Are not the sky's astrologies but forms
Of knowledge. Flotillas of green grass
Fill up with towns of stone as we retire—
Pitiful sculptures housing our disguise.
Lady,
    nature only arrives.

3
Since tired nature is indifferent to
Coins, coliseums, Elizabethan plays,
And forms of knowledge, lady, arrive,
And be, like the astrological swan,
A magic affinity of appetite.

The sea is filled with sunsets and reveals
What largely starves us: the complacencies
Of habit—not the mirrors and delights
Of pleasure, but the lying sticks and stones
Of loveless days on lovely days for love.

The sea is stonily indifferent to
The otherness of blurred flotillas. We
Antonyms of nature are as weeds because
Our graves are natural and evil, yet
Green grass will house us and be serviceable.

The rivers' treasuries fight nature to
The sea; in stones, astrologies reveal
Their sculpturing, as if the sky, disguised,
Lay pitifully banked in gravel; palms
Remain along the river-banks, while towns

Grow starved on what enlarges them. When we
Dance, synthetic in intensity,
Starved on nature, starving on ourselves,
Delight may be sky-writing on the sky,
Lady,
        only nature arrives.

Three Winter Poems

1

Slowly among the ampersands
Of snow crisping the hair's net
With *and, and*—and steel air
Taking its helmet off, I walked
Out past the lights of great hotels,
Grillwork trees, and former farms,
Into the sway of family scenes:
Those nests that will not let me go.

2

How could long walkers ever know
That they are walking to be still,
Cold step by cold step?
It is too bad that fires end—
Cinders, embers, ashes—all
Animate vividness born to stop,
Snowy mile on snowy mile.

3

Was that you flying down a flight of stairs
Into a thousand snowflakes of goodbye?
How many chronic pastures churned
Under a windfall, all so calm
Above, with the landscape pinned down,
Layer on layer, beneath the snow,
Whose wide, white, implacable gesso
Was preparing itself for snow, more snow
(The painting under the painting), for
Those days that yet might come to bloom.

Hunting and Fishing

Who are you, love, who haunts the northern sphere?
Ghost of the shore, or lost desert walker,
Once flesh and blood, I took you in my arms,
The sheets turned over all their lakes and snows,
Four ungloved hands like hunters at their furs
No thicket overlooked, and no hedgerows,

Or, as the fisher over water goes,
We bent to bait the universal trout
Below, its silver scales our runabout;
Caught, pursuit ended, and ended travel
When breath sped blood to all its ports of call,
Angel who fell to nothing through a hole.

Bay Days

1

The clouds were doing unoriginal things
With grandeur yesterday, moving paintings
From here to there, slowly dispersing
Gangs of angels. Today there's nothing,
Nothing but a camera taking nothing.
Summer. Weather. Nothing could be clearer.
It is a perfect day, with no cloud cover.

2

The birds' gradual declension stops.
The darkness takes the longest time to darken.
Sums of stars add to the overhead.
A city of hunches thickens and grows thin,
Appears and disappears across the water,
Depending on the light's strange gift for hanging
Scenery. And then for taking it down.

3

Each night, the outlines of that city form
Films of the ideal, illuminations
Of crumpled battlements whose rising argot
Is faintly heard above the motorboats;
Here, the night philosophers break camp
Down to a single-minded tent of parting.
The fire's out. The animals are gone.

4

Currents always running, gauged to light
And wind, the depths varying the colors:

A copper milky green, an ink-splash blue
Turned tinsel. A vain castle's sinking
Into its sewerage system. A particle of sail,
Hurrying to meet its particle of sun,
Shakes the whole slack surface into speed.

5
Decisive laboring: the composition
The rain was trying to compose this morning
On what the sun had glossed as marginalia.
References to happiness are obsolete
According to the gloomy view this evening,
Which says existence is the only share
Of joy that's ever in our ardent power.

6
I tried today to make of the wild roses
An untimely bouquet. Opening, falling,
They never last long—in short, they're dying.
Now I am thinking of taking to drinking
Earlier than usual. Gin. And something.
A potion of petals. They're thorns by evening.
Wild roses in the trash can in the morning.

Travel: A Window

I think it's possible
To stare
Too long through a window
At birch trees
Until their negatives
Displace the rare,
Handwritten white bark's
Peeling pieces,

To leave your house
For a summer seizure
Of blue and find,
Instead of its weather,
A lean wolf sitting
Back on his haunches
On widening snow,

Above him a sparrow
Cold in the
Insufferable branches.

Saratoga

Who would dream there is a street of Chasidic Jews
Left over among the mineral waters,
Black-bearded, black, among the cures of summer,
In rows of rooming houses gone to seed
Braced by vines in which they seem suspended?

This is a country of seconds—a kind
Of bucolic, demented Garment District:
Landscapes and yardgoods going for a song—
Windfalls of shirts on the cheap at the mill,
Factories where hands still touch the fabric.

The hills are overstocked with sunsets.
Cemeteries—are they housing projects
For never enough? Or too much of everything?
So this is the end of animals and dancers!
Poor brain, talking to a barn of dust!

In the dowdy beautiful Victorian dark
Of the steamy park's old brick and shadow,
Dilapidated concrete drowsy troughs,
Like laboratory tanks for mosquito larvae,
Piddle away brown-ferned scummed water.

How to be a beach resort without an ocean
Suggests the theme. The subject's certain:
The slower the town the more obsessed by speed.
Between the ballet dancers of July,
The dramatic, high-strung August chargers

Surely some point must be being drawn!
Stirred up overnight: the swank emulsion
Of the rich, the corrupt, the merely sporting—
Dressy traders of expensive horseflesh,
Statues of jockeys upright on the lawn.

The Nineteenth Century is in the trees.
Down at the horse barns at night, the yearlings—
Part cricket field, part Arabian strains—
Wait to be named. Tradition . . . bargains.
Old tastes deplore the lost amenities.

Muscle under silk lifts the dancer's Swan,
Spurs the leggy velvet colt of speed—
Power gathered in the glacial rock fault
Tempting vision with what it cannot see:
Fresh water running toward immortal salt.

After the Ballet

(Saratoga, July 4)

Where do the dancers go after dancing,
The tumult of the action slowly fading,
Asterisk, bulb, and incandescent
Roman candle rushing into starlight?
Where do the watchers go after dancing,
The crowds of people dim in the stage light?
The rockets of celebration wildly
Flare for a moment, dangle and darken.

Shorelines

Someday I'll wake and hardly think of you;
You'll be some abstract deity, a myth—
Say Daphne, if you knew her as a tree.
Don't think I won't be grateful. I will be.
We'd shuck the oysters, cool them off with lime,
Spice them with Tabasco, and then scoop them up,
Who thought we were in Paradise. We were not.
Three couples and three singles shared that house
For two weeks in September. Wellfleet stayed
Remarkable that fall. And so did we.
Confessions, confidences kept us up
Half the night; the dawn birds found us still
Dead tired, clenched on the emotional,
Which led to two divorces later on,
Recriminations, torn-up loyalties,
The dreariness of things gone wrong for good.
Yet who could forget those wet, bucolic rides,
Drunk dances on the beach, the bonfires,
The sandy lobsters not quite fit to eat?
Well, there were other falls to come as bad,
But I still see us on a screened-in porch,
Dumbly determined to discover when
The tide turned and the bay sank back in mud.
We'd watch it carefully, hour after hour,
But somehow never could decide just when
The miracle occurred. Someone would run
Into the marshes yelling, "Where's the shore?"
We hardly see each other anymore.

On Route 202, New Hampshire

Winter's patchwork being slapped on again
Drubs a young birch to the ground. Spring's thaw
Will uncover this year's dead dog. These old
Mill towns with their French-Canadian names
Still stock the remainders: a Rochambeau
Holds the snowmobile franchise, a Toussé
Runs a run-down sort of *boulangerie*
Down by the river, which is black with leaves.
Discrepancies grow worse when posed against
The mountains, calm but exhilarating,
Repeating their lesson over and over:
Beautiful scenery is never insolvent.

Saturday night in a steepled snow town,
A line is forming at the bowling alley.
Across the street, a tropical fish store
Exhibits its not very exotic items:
Circulating flags of dispirited color,
Small fry glumly running in their tanks,
As if they deplored where chance had placed them—
Somewhere between New York and Boston.

Nearing the Lights

You are nearing the lights, either at
A window or on a road, you are
Watching the skyline right itself,
Or, coming into a town, you are

Watching the nearness somewhere else
Of early supper at a farm,
Or, in a town I'd never know,
Somewhere the lights are coming on,

Somewhere the night is holding out
And onto a river and a tree.
Is it the dusk or candlewick
Aflame or streetlamp that I see

Wavering, steadying, drawing near
Worlds that the day gives up to dark?
The moon puts down its gangplank in the sea
As if pure light could disembark.

Equivocal starlight turns into
Blank sky, then daylight. I see you
There at a window or in a car,
Where, in nearing the light, you are.

V

Buried City

If you have come, expecting miracles . . .
But you I need not warn. We worked for years
Only to arrive at deeper mysteries:
This cave, for instance, these rarities.
Notice the wall painting, strangest of all;
The hunter hunts himself, his animal—
Can you make it out, its pure illusion?

We've had it reproduced a hundred ways:
Reversed, blown-up, mirror-reversed, X-rayed,
Reduced, and so forth. Still we're in the dark.
And here, look close, an alphabet of shards—
Two perfect halves of shell, one broken one,
Intended, we believe, to signify
The pairings of the soul, the harm of love.

Some slanted stag—perhaps a buffalo
With horns above a human face, a spear
Pointing to its childlike heart and held
In . . . what? Paws? Fingers of a hand?—may be
A suicide at bay. Behind, a tree,
Half drawn to light and yet quite shadowy
Proves the more we look the less we see.

And so the very subject of the painting still
Remains an enigma. I have stared at it
As if I were in love with its other side,
A silversmith inside a mirror, say,
Inventing winter, or a snowman turned

Into a figure-skater on the moon—
These icy images too soon give way

To tropical motifs: a diver in
A South Seas coral-blue lagoon—you know
Those afternoons we never think about
Until we're there in animal sunlight . . .
To be a diver and a scholar both
And not divided into north and south—
Could that be the painting's ambiguous myth?

Now we know that what we do not know
Stamps its print upon the brain in shadow,
A kind of Hegelian doubletalk
Has wrung the neck of all things straight. Behind
The mask its opposite, and so on. Where
The surface says all living things are one,
A deep disunity botches the design.

Imagine the rehearsals of the mad,
A stormswept gully where dead cats rain down
On peasants praying for food and water,
The inextinguishable pain of children
Destroyed by what can never happen. Think
Of houses, dinners, all mendacious calm,
Then, rising at the edge of Paradise, a slum

In whose bleak tenements some poor souls sit
Forever, staring into a machine,
Muttering about youth. A young girl, sick

At heart, keeps travelling through a town
Projected on a screen (of which she's unaware);
Trying to get to the other side each time,
And always failing, she begins again.

The painting is changing from this angle. Watch.
Among surrealist bits of paint and flame,
Coal barges burn themselves to water music,
Crass winter hazards clutter the spring stream,
Boats float past, reflected upside-down,
As if the malignant bridges of the town
Formed full circles—an optical illusion,

Along with many others. It's just one step
From the banquet hall to the garbage dump
And most of life is on the routes between.
We love high notes, expensive memories,
One more giant among the concertos,
Whose soloist needs rescuing from time to time
From heights on which he's suddenly stranded.

The sound of a light breather took us years
To trace, a joke of sorts too close to home;
At first the syllables were jumbled, words
Toppled on each other till we made them out:
Whispered art lectures, obscene taunts, and then
The sound of footsteps, running, running,
The breath of someone suddenly choked off.

Terror is a rumor till it grinds on fact:

Once more the threat of the internment camps
Drilled inside a mountain—somebody's ironic
Little hole-in-one. Wry memory games
Are not sufficient to explain how cruel
Power is, and was, and always will be—
You name the one perfected revolution

Whose ends and means didn't separate in time!
The painting might symbolize the war between
Social classes, the ego and the id,
Black and white, man and woman, heart and spleen . . .
Or illustrate how God is territory,
Or could it be an anagram?—"You know . . .?"
     "I mean . . .?"
An early myth the shells are meant to story?

Prevailing easterlies, the winds that sit
In the hills beyond the roofs are ready to blow
Even this museum to salty pieces.
The sails rise up like salvaged dirty laundry,
The cranks churn rust, and off we go again,
This time slightly askew, and slowly—
Once more turned away from the nearby harbor.

Baked in lava, the figures at Pompeii
Were art imitating life, and vice
Versa. Lovers locked in stone became
Worldwide pornography, a warning sign
To make ye haste, the rosebuds are soon gone;
Graffiti on the walls read *mene, mene,*
Tekel, upharsin—and the city fell.

And with it went the logs of fine apparel,
The rangy autumn days of walks and smoke,
The silver flanks of rock, the sulphur smudges
Floating on the bog's abandoned grasses
Housing a million forms of crawling life
That rose in gauze among the spring allotments—
Life so rich it oiled the hinge of feeling—

But when the city went, so did the country.
It's possible the painting is that world
Too soon pockmarked, diseased with furrows, or
Conversely mountained with the hilly scales
Of greasy patches of a sickness where
Beauty once had claimed a sure perfection—
Civil order crumbled into fiction?

Caveat emptor. Caves are everywhere:
Eye-pit, labyrinth of ear, skull-hollow,
Cavern of the grave. What appetite arouses
Pleasure defiles in age's tittle-tattle.
From here on in, we synchronize our watches,
For looking at paintings is a form of waiting
And time's the one disease everybody catches.

The wards of poverty remain the real
Real estate of history: Butchers share
Rooms at the top, those little royal roosts—
The King's chair here, the Queen's chair there;
Implicit hierarchies worked into the plan
Reveal the obvious: Envy, a small town,
Grew into the housing project of the world.

And yet that cemetery Valéry
Glazed into a permanent rooftop shimmer
Endures . . . but as a poem or a reality?
Even the truest of philosophies
Founders on the death of the philosopher.
The sea's a grave. A graveyard at the sea
Occasions, and subverts, the poetry.

Slowly this buried city came to light.
Up from the ruins, all its riddles blank
(Its verses, too), with no one to look out
While all of us looked in. We were the mere
Observers, really, not the partisans
Of life. At the exit, sign the pledge
Forbidding you to say that we exist at all.

Let them not wash in the wake of the uttering
Seagulls or blind themselves white on embankments
Of chalk or devour the dry egg of madness . . .
That thin-ribbed pattern on the wall revives
A city in the brain, its choked canals,
Its crowded terminals . . . We're rising through
Levels of thought where dark and light converge.

And now the World . . . We've reached the upper air.
Goodbye, goodbye . . . The deer stop dead to hear
The first retort of gunshots in the wood.
Exiled from exile, you will always bear
Two sacred marks of the interior:
Memory and art. How early it grows dark!
They say the snow will bury us this year.

Howard Moss

Howard Moss is the poetry editor of *The New Yorker*.
Before joining its staff in 1948, he was an instructor
of English at Vassar College. The author of eight
books of poems, including this one, and two books
of criticism, *The Magic Lantern of Marcel Proust* and
Writing Against Time, he has also edited the poems of
Keats, the nonsense verse of Edward Lear, and a
collection of short stories written by poets, *The
Poet's Story*. A play, *The Folding Green*, was first
produced by The Poets' Theater in Cambridge, Mass.,
and then by The Playwrights' Unit in New York
City, and a more recent work, *The Palace at 4 A.M.*,
was produced in the summer of 1972 at the John
Drew Theater in East Hampton, with Edward Albee
as its director. In the same year, Moss received the
National Book Award for his *Selected Poems*. In 1974,
he published a book of satirical biographies, *Instant
Lives*, with drawings by Edward Gorey. Moss is a
member of The National Institute of Arts and Letters
and received a grant in creative writing from that
organization in 1968.